As we continue to live through our world's "chain of unbearable events," it is time for the sharp and sweet audacity of Ewa Chrusciel's work. You don't have to believe a person can become a bird to adore Ewa Chrusciel's nwwwew book, but I dare you to read it without considering it might be true. The book is poetry because you'll find yourself considering not just that it might happen, but how. Using the world of birds, *Yours, Purple Gallinule* shows us, in observations and witticisms crisp as the bite of an apple, the limits of our own understanding, as it directs us towards new possibilities we can be grateful for. Paired with illustrations by Nancy Sepe that marry playfulness and sorrow, *Yours, Purple Gallinule* is both light and dark, comedy and tragedy, agile at both: what Robert Frost would call "play for mortal stakes."

—Katie Peterson, author of *Life in a Field*

In *Yours, Purple Gallinule*, Ewa Chrusciel invites us to fall in with birds and be astonished by an aclosural world of mental aviaries and "tiny throat" diagnoses. Like the poet herself, who is a descendant of birds, our souls are "winged". Thus we are transported to a liminal world of mythmaking and identity formation by embracing derangement and creating our own migration. *Yours, Purple Gallinule* brims with humor, erudition, and, yes!, heresy. It dazzles with a fierce imagination and is a superb addition to Ewa Chrusciel's already impressive body of work.

—Abayomi Animashaun, author of *Seahorses*

"A baby titmouse is tucking itself under my elbow," Poet Ewa Chrusciel says in the first line of her boldly ambitious fourth collection, *Yours, Purple Gallinule*, in which she weaves an inextricable connection between the lives of birds and our own spiritual and physical lives. Chrusciel wrestles with the definition and meaning of poetry and its relationship to

imagination, psychic disorder, fragmentation, exile and history: "A poem is a ravenous flock of snow buntings, an apocalypse of the air. Mad in its dazzlement," she notes. Hundreds of birds sing, shit, nest, shed feathers, hide in crevices, mount defenses, create families, search for food for their babies, and soar in these pages. *Yours, Purple Gallinule* is a book of migrations and transformations, astounding facts and revelations—wise and utterly original.

—Jeff Friedman, author of *The Marksman* and *Floating Tales*

In *Yours, Purple Gallinule* Ewa Chrusciel focuses her keen poetic eye on the order to be found inside psychiatric disorders. The speaker in these poems is a psychiatrist using the guidelines of *The Diagnostic and Statistical Manual of Mental Disorders* to diagnose and treat birds. Applying the intensely intellectual to the truly primal, Chrusciel opens an intriguing new space for our consideration. In that space the taxonomical, mystic, and clinical merge and hum along with unique energy and fresh lyricism. As with Ewa's other works, there is a deep look into one of our current cultural problems—attitudes toward mental health. The book is filled with the illuminating discoveries that we all hope to find when reading poetry. Readers benefit from the surprise and depth of these strange and wonderful poems.

—Maudelle Driskell, The director of The Frost Place and author of *Talismans*

Ewa Chrusciel

Illustrated by Nancy Sepe

Cover and interior art by Nancy Sepe

Cover typeface: Avenir
Interior typfaces: Adobe Minion Pro & Myriad Pro

Interior design by Ken Keegan

Library of Congress Cataloging-in-Publication Data

Names: Chruściel, Ewa, author.
Title: Yours, purple gallinule / Ewa Chrusciel.
Description: Oakland, California : Omnidawn Publishing, [2022] | Summary:
  "Ewa Chrusciel's fourth book in English, Yours, Purple Gallinule,
  playfully explores health and illness as they are culturally
  constructed. Using research about various bird species, clinical
  understandings of mental afflictions and their treatment through
  history, Chrusciel maps various diagnostics onto an array of avian
  species. Intended as a lyrical satire, the book is a reflection on a
  society that tends to over-diagnose, misdiagnose, over-medicate. Among
  the questions these poems ask is: What does it mean to be unique, to
  accept pain and suffering as a fact of life? On the pages of Yours,
  Purple Gallinule, we encounter birds, a poet, and a psychiatrist who
  diagnoses birds with various mental afflictions. The psychiatrist
  undergoes a series of conversions as she realizes that the point is not
  to classify thoughtlessly, but to "make music instead"-to dwell in
  astonishment. Birds evade the anthropomorphization of psychiatrists -
  and of poets - when psychiatrist and poet become one. The
  anthropomorphization goes in reverse, and the human being becomes more
  "other," more avian. Like Noah's dove, it proclaims a new covenant, with
  a twig in its beak and a message: "We are all mad; some more than
  others, but no one is spared the affliction. And the madder we are, the
  more sacred.""-- Provided by publisher.

Identifiers: LCCN 2022034932 | ISBN 9781632431103 (trade paperback)
Subjects: LCGFT: Poetry.
Classification: LCC PS3603.H78 Y68 2022 | DDC 811/.6--dc23/eng/20220721
LC record available at https://lccn.loc.gov/2022034932

Published by Omnidawn Publishing, Oakland, California
www.omnidawn.com   (510) 237-5472
10 9 8 7 6 5 4 3 2 1
ISBN: 978-1-63243-110-3

Silliness, absurdity, and freedom are distinct in their lineage but arguably reside in the same cladogram.

Eric DeLuca

My soul is a sacred bird, the Highest Heaven its nest:
Fretting within the body's bars, it finds on earth no rest

Hafiz

Table Of Contents

Tiny Throat Foreword:

The birds chirp: *There are more feathers, shells, and songs in heaven and earth, Humans, than are dreamt of in your diagnostic manuals.*

A baby titmouse is tucking itself under my elbow. Its beak ajar to let out a tiny snore. I remove it gently; I need to type notes from my session with the Himalayan griffon. But it resists and tucks itself under my chin. I keep writing with my head bent to the right, which makes my notes rhythmic. Other tits arrive – they scatter the paper, attacking the ink bottle with beaks. I keep stashes of cheese and nuts in my drawer. Three tits adopt a skidding approach: The breeze of giddy wings flutters my pages and for a split second paper birds join the game. They are fascinated by the law of gravity and they push the pencils from my desk. I see curiosity in their eyes, a tiny-winged idea: "Why do these long creatures, dressed as trees and metallic tails not take off?" They pierce the pencils to see if they will rise. They don't. Tired of the gravity game, they outstretch their wings on the part of the paper where the Sun falls. They lie now flat on their breast with beaks half open – sunbathing. I decide to nap. They notice the change of my position and move to my pillow to slide down on their butts with their legs outstretched. I get back to my desk and open my drawer with cheese. One tit gets hold of a cheese morsel first; the others chase him. They swarm and squeak and emit swear notes…

Flames in their eyes – ruffled feathers – tits on the floor now – feet overlocked, rolling around – shrill notes – feathers flying.

14

Cedar waxwings

They eat crabapples in one tree and poop seeds onto another. We can rule out hypochondria.

"You are really cool birds," I say, "worthy of a book, or at least a poem. Why don't you poop where the fruit is? Maybe you don't want to pollute your food?"

The tree wants you to go somewhere else. There is nothing wrong with you, I think, except your uniqueness. The *tree* might be a bit OCD.

A poem is a ravenous flock of snow buntings, an apocalypse of the air. Mad in its dazzlement. How did they get here? Prancing gleefully, feeding on a poem's madness. At certain times they are flakes of snow – diamonds shimmering, all facets at once, migrant words flashing. Other times, they resemble giant bees, hungry for virgins and sinners, and too otherworldly for prose.

If the poem is a snow bunting? Winding, treacherous – you need to wrestle it like Jacob did the Angel. Its otherness will bless, and wound.

Tiny Throat Diagnoses

Marabou stork, you vandalized my office. Your criminalization is coterminous with your victimization. It is repetition compulsion. Other storks bring babies; you defecate on your own legs after killing pretty flamingoes. Freud (now extinct) called this process primary ego defense.

Knobbed Hornbill invites a female in a nest and then plugs the entrance with excreta and mud. Only a slit remains through which she can poop. It is for safety reasons, he claims, to defend her from monkeys.

Do we imitate birds or birds, us? A mama hornbill seals herself in with her own poop and stays two months to protect her young. Her nose is a ponderous tool for accruing dung.

As a child I used to smell my panties. My mother smiled and told me: *A hoopoe chick will throw urine in your face if you poke its nest.*

Tiny Throat Diagnoses:
White Ptarmigan

When you flew into my office, you became my papers. I even carried you home by mistake and when I opened my satchel, the pages fluttered and hissed. What to say? You know no boundaries. Your plumage is camouflage. You become snow. You are a flock of Dominican monks carving on skis. You are a mogul.

Are you a split self? Watch *Zelig*. Do you feel alone in the most complete way?

Cupping

On the solemn occasion of my pneumonia,
my mother performs the ritual of cupping,
bańki, in Polish. She brings me tiny torches,
lights a match
and heats up each glass
cup and sucks it to my back.

New colonies pop up
with chiefs and warriors:
Soon there are volcanoes, flesh
erupting into valleys.
My back bubbling in seismic shifts.

Black ash shed
ring by ring, a loon in distant waters
sings.

They vanish and return
in ripples of red

Tiny Throat Diagnoses

I hear a commotion. The bird council has a great titmouse in handcuffs. He ate a sparrow's brain. They want to know if I can evaluate him.

Following a hunch, I browse through the files of sibilants: swans, swifts, Sumatran bulbul, shortwing, shoveler, smoky honeyeater, snowfinch, shrike, spurfowl, sparrowhawk, striped tit babbler… Here we go: house sparrow; known to be a bully.

You see, titmice are creatures of habit. They always roost at 6 pm. The sparrow disturbed his routine.

I explain this backstory to the council and advise them to send the titmouse to a training on how to deal with aggression.

Notes from the Mental Aviary - I

(In India a dog demon causes madness. Horace called depression, "black dog." So did Winston Churchill. Another term is "wolf madness."

Babylonians and Mesopotamians believed in spirit invasion. Christianity has a tradition of linking madness to possession. But Voltaire, Diderot and Freud, considered Christianity as madness. Ancient Greeks had a rational approach to illness. As long as a man curbed his appetites, he was free from insanity.

Erasmus wrote *In Praise of Folly*. To call a poet mad was a compliment.)

A woodcock sits horizontally
for a long time
until it spirals up
and zigzags down, peent-ing into silence

and I suffer vertigo.

A blue titmouse taps. Her flight is so spic-and-span! But she utters panic notes. I step outside and she leads me to a branch where her sultan tit sits, stunned. Misiu (my cat) must have turned him catatonic.

A few hours later, the sultan tit is on the opposite side of catatonic. Angry glitter in his eyes, he is about to slit my cat's white throat. He's had it with both of us.

His spouse rallied all the neighborhood tits. They stake a claim: The birds have written a petition – if I want to continue my practice, I can't keep cats; it is two-faced.

Tiny Throat Diagnoses:
The Oven cannot hear the ovenbird

I put out my feeder to attract nightingales, but I get ovenbirds instead. '*tea-Cher, tea-Cher, tea-CHER, Tea-CHER, TEA-CHER*' – a tedious song. Not the trills and jitters. A sexless song, wrenched out of want. Tough little lives of ovenbirds, half the adults die. They never see their work. They sing forty songs, like rainy days, and then kaput. They leave layers of riddles, odes, villanelles, and a dismembered tune. A tedious tedious song.

Lord, why did you make me an ovenbird?

Little sad ovenbird, I could prescribe you an antidepressant, but isn't it better to write these poems of good, better, and pooped out? Poems of shadow that fall between a song, and an *idea* of a song?

Notes from the Mental Aviary - II

(Boring holes in the skull to release demons dates back to 5000 BC. Ancients intuited that illness comes from evil. Greeks believed in divine madness, but also disease. Hippocrates: A too-hot or too-cold mind... He attributed melancholy to black bile. Blood, phlegm, yellow bile and black bile... If these fluids are in the right proportion, we are healthy. But a *dyscrasia* (bad mixture) means illness. People with red blood are friendly and have pretty skin. People with yellow bile are bitter, aggressive. People with black bile are sad, despondent. They have black eyes and hair. People with phlegm...)

Tiny Throat Diagnoses

Swallows, you don't stop for sex? Belly to belly, 2,000 feet in the air?
Are you an exhibitionist or an idealist? After the deed, you spiral
down, together, faster than an aircraft, and then detach to avoid
crashing into the earth. Has your corpus striatum been damaged?

Mongols would take towns by fire, tying incendiary materials to
your tails. At the helm, Genghis Khan took entire cities that way by
igniting 10,000 of your relatives.

We could prescribe bloodsuckers, though I'm a bit concerned Pliny
might suggest a ducking chair.

Lunacies

Flickers signing trees with their initials.
Frigate birds napping in midair,
inflating a red pouch into a balloon.
House finches nesting in cigarette butts,
kites using stolen underwear.
Ibises, scarlet from eating so many crabs.
Bassian thrushes farting into dirt
to unearth the worms.
Woodcocks duck-walking,
Waxwings drunk from fermented fruit.
Crows sledding on roofs in plastic bags.
Cranes clawing a stone to ward off sleep.

Tiny Throat Diagnoses

I have been listening to you, dear loon.

I hear in your trilling a melancholy.
You inherited melancholy from your grandparents. How do you
regulate the states of your system? Neurotransmitters? How do you
restore your humoral equilibrium?

The point – entelechy? A relationship between real and potential,
with astonishment of feathers.

Notes from the Mental Aviary - III

(Hildegard of Bingen – a medieval Benedictine visionary – equates black bile with Adam and Eve's sin. The apple brought on melancholia. A demonic origin… Hildegard states: *This black bile is dark and bitter and spews out every evil, sometimes even [causing] an infirmity of the brain… [H]uman beings can feel no joy about the heavenly life and can take no comfort in their present life… The demons hurry to this painful affliction, [as] madness is one of their tasks.*

Hildegard recommends eating the liver of ostrich to cure melancholia.)

Acts of Exile

My 80-year-old dad visits from his native country. The Global Café club I run at the college is having a belly-dancing workshop. There is a table with some soda and chips for the workshop guests.

The workshop begins and my father positions himself in an armchair far in the corner with a bowlful of chips.

It is the first time I am taking a belly-dancing workshop.
It is his first encounter with chips. The chips, a symbol of the rotten West, were inaccessible during the Communist Regime. After the Regime collapsed, they were one of the most expensive imports on Polish shelves.

I bend the knee to drop the hip and straighten the knee to lift the hip again and again. My dad in his corner lifts each chip to his mouth and crunches, over and over. Not unlike a burlesque show, we each indulge in the forbidden.

The belly-dancing coach says:
Imagine you have your arms full of groceries and you push the car door shut with your hip. I recall my dad getting lost, years ago, his first time in an American supermarket.
I imagine him hiding there until they close the shop; wandering between the aisles and snacking from every possible shelf.

Now he is my only child in the corner of the room, an empty bowl in his hands. Later that day, he will tell me he is not hungry and won't have dinner.

The closer you are to the ground, the easier it will be for you to find the balance, the coach says.

How we both try.

Tiny Throat Diagnoses

Chick-a-dee-dee-dee, a psychopath in the skin of innocence. At night you sneak into hollow trees and peck at bats' heads – which you eat later. Your brain might be too moist. Do you ever succumb to despondency?

In my research on your case, I've noted that your theropod relatives [dinosaurs all] dieted from 163 kilos to 1. They wanted to fit better into tiny trees.

I've come to believe you are who you are through miniaturization.

A Dozen Larks stormed into my office carrying seven clouds. And I don't mean cumulus, stratus, and cirrus. These didn't even look like clouds of unknowing. They were beyond incomprehensible— ineffable. They were not made of human alphabet.

In the meantime, the larks rolled like scrolls around the pins of their own laughter. What were they laughing about? They were simply disciples of joy.

But I was in a straightjacket. I noted down: "They sing at inappropriate times – in my office, for example, where I conduct serious research."

Notes from the Mental Aviary - IV

(Medievalists believed madness was caused by a stone in one's head. Fixed ideas cause delusions. Hieronymus Bosch painted "Extracting the Stone of Madness" in 1457, which reenacts a trephination.

Weltschmerz, world-pain...
After Goethe wrote *The Sorrows of Young Werther,* there was a spike in suicides and young people wore black cloaks.)

The Poet Reads Aloud Bishop's "Moose" to Her Students

I trot line-by-line showing my students
leaps in space and time.
Poetry is an arctic fox – I tell them –
leaping in the air
to catch his prey. Each of his muscles
astute. Fox eats like a saint.

When I get to the bus's sudden jolt,
as the moose comes out of impenetrable woods,
Towering, antlerless, high as a church, homely as a house
I want them to be there, to get a match struck in the dark.

But all my students hear from my eastern European accent
is *mouse*. What's the big deal, why stop the bus, they whisper.
& the mouse as big as a church…?

They wonder at my love of poetry, my silly enthusiasm.
& I think of all my life ambitions –
as big as Caucasus mountains to me,
mounds to others.

& how I want to rise in the middle of the road
like a cathedral, stop passersby,
but all they see is a small mouse,
nervously building her nests
in foreign walls.

Notes from the Mental Aviary - V

(In liminal places such as waters, rivers, and seas, monsters reside. The mad sea hosts water snakes and luring sirens. The sea has no map. But human beings are classifying creatures: we want puzzles to be solved. Hence, the DSM. We lose our mind without closures. Madness, a lack of order, too strange to be classified.

A link between madness and nothingness... Was it Adam and Eve clinging to a false promise? Does *horror vacui* lead to madness? Or, to its institutionalization, in Foucault's words, "great confinement"? A roaming holy fool –
canceled, relegated to an enclosure, a cage. Does humanity debase the mad, because they scream *humanity*? Are they too much? Don Quixote – mad, because he is human. So is Dostoevsky's Idiot. Madness from too much love, unrequited love and love gone awry, the loss of a beloved, a bubble of love, a betrayal.)

History of (a Goldfinch's) Madness

Turkish smugglers caught him in the wild
and trapped him in a veiled cage,
hung in a cafe.
Deprived of light,
the goldfinch mourned, his song
a prayer of lament. Sorrow breeds melodies.
Pipe smoke wafted through the room.
The men meditated; they puffed nostalgic rings
into the air. The goldfinches' plaintive song
lingered and soared, towards mates and meadows.
What will light up these darkened souls?
We perfect our yearning in death.
For the lack of a God, we distill visions
from tiny throats.

Notes from the Mental Aviary - VI

(In *History of Madness*, Foucault says when lepers left, "deranged minds" took their place. Madmen were exiled; sometimes publicly whipped and offered to sailors. Water purifies. That's how the *Narrenschiff* originated, the ship of fools, carrying them away from the boundaries of the earth. The sea has no limits. Violent immersion in cold water was a treatment for witches...

Madness leads to confinement, or confinement to madness....?

The ship of fools – a fancy literary trope. Now there are the inflatable boats of refugees, reaching – or not – island asylums.

On the top of Bosch's mast, an owl resides.)

Tiny Throat Diagnoses

The bird comes in with an unrecognizable tril tr p prrrtr sszśź
The notes are arrhythmic. It misunderstands other birdcalls. Frantic,
neurotic. Rather hard to detect – looks like some cross between an
American robin and a European sparrow – drab colors. Due to its
mental state, no doubt.

It has no affiliations.

It must have crossed some borders. It's a bird with an accent. No avian
passport (or it's expired).

Look, bird, you shuffle your tunes from one flora to another. Most
birds are migrants but the trajectory's clear: *home* – dumpster field or
South American rainforests – *back home*. Here, we have a disruptive
path of cliffs and lacunas. *Horror vacui.*

The bird tries harder than others. Restless, ever adapting, its flashes of
paranoia are clues to the dictatorship it once fled.

I offer meds. It refuses. I offer a migration-displacement support
group. I invite backyard birds over; we perch in a circle. We use
an app: *Create your own migration.* They fill the fields, which get
projected onto a board. The communal experience is grand—we are
all on the same flight. But the border bird keeps apart.

It will take a solitary flight. Why should it settle for less, sell its soul
for affluent demons of pharmaceuticals? The more it buffets the wind,
the stronger its wings will be.

A bird who *is*
shadows the one
who *pretends* to be.
The mystic runs to the Holy Water
to scatter marigold petals, and ashes.

Notes from the Mental Aviary - VII

(A naked man stuck in the crest of a giant hoopoe, perching like a
voyeur. A bird with clay jars on its legs devouring a man from whose
ass tarred swallows fly. The dybbuks of birds nest in our brains.
New branches sprout; quills proliferate. Each soul gnarls into lines,
intertwines with syllables on a frozen lake. Two laughing storks strut
their acrobatic legs. The lost hedgehog casts its thorny crown.
Does the desire or its suppression breed pestilence?
Bosch's birds incarnate madness).

Consider a Womb as a Bird

One powder blue unfertilized egg
and three blue nestlings
& we build a station of dreams:
fecundity, what is it?
If she had a child, she would tell it
these nesting boxes are about luck & timing
although best when they just transpire:
So we can proclaim a miracle
and shun meticulous planning.

But she tells an invisible child
carrying her down rivers
that to be the mother
of all means to dwell in sorrow
& evanescence.

A mother and a virgin in One is our
ideal, so we overcome gravity with tales.

And these bluebirds, domesticated
partially, reproduce in our hands.

Hands of a mother are a cradle,
and hands of a non-gravitational mother –
a boat.

Ancient Greeks believed the uterus
had suckers. Imagine
it as an octopus
or a cuttlefish.

And that brings us to wetness.
The nature of mother and the ocean are one.

A womb – animal within animal –
and because we are only to understand analogically,
a womb is also a vessel, wineskin, and a dove.

Holy Spirit. Fallopian tubes as wings.
That's why shamans dress as birds
to access the other world. What flutters.

Notes from the Mental Aviary - VIII

In 1766, Hannah Mackenzie of London was confined to an insane asylum by her husband because she objected to him stealing her money and having an affair with her niece.

Women were punished by their fathers or husbands for violating boundaries: Elizabeth, wife of a Calvinist pastor, was institutionalized for three years by force for opposing his radicalism. A doctor disguised himself as a sewing machine salesman, won Elizabeth's confidence, and confined her for refusing to shake his hand. The proof of insanity. When she returned from the asylum, her husband locked her in the house. Eventually, she broke free and started the Anti-Insane Asylum Society.

I Called a Grief Support Group the Other Day

How long has it been since your loss? A man asked.
No specific date, I said. It happened imperceptibly,
through slow shrinking. There were no funeral rites,
only tiny articles missing, confusing parts of speech,
making up my own words. Mourning my mother
tongue. I called friends' eyebrows—eyebushes.
Or I would brood over them, unable to decide
which words to choose. Do you feel abandoned
by God? The voice on the other line asked.
How could I? I speak in tongues now, but they flicker
in the air – they burn me at the tip and vanish.
Perhaps you could plant a tree
or write a poem? The man asked in conclusion,
as he had to attend to other deaths.

Whisper through an eggshell.
A chick will whisper back
ring by ring – we shed ash
to know our dreams.
A loon in distant water
weeps.

Notes from the Mental Aviary - IX

To remedy madness (Hildegard says):

Take laurel berries and pulverize them. Then take wheat flour, combine it with laurel powder and mix it with blessed-thistle water. After the patient's head has been shaved, spread it and hold it in place with a felt cap until he's warmed. Repeat often and the patient will regain his senses.

Notes from the Mortal Aviary - IX

Tiny Throat Diagnoses

Southern cassowary, you arrive when your feathers are tinged with spurs. I must decipher your ventriloquist booms. Your body shudders and you complain about the anticonvulsants they put you on. Well, you slapped your spouse and you attacked the village doctor. Never mind your spouse is obsessed with hand sanitizer. You kick doors and windows – self-hate – you attack your reflection. Yet some villagers will trade you for a wife…

The village council suggests I dissect your cranium.
I tell them claw-boxing can bring birds closer.

I prescribe Leibnizian metaphysics, Augustine's *Confessions*, and bromine.

A Poet and a Shrink (I)

When does the poet start diagnosing birds and the psychiatrist
start writing poems? What is their diagnosis? Grandiosity, trauma
and borderline poetry, carpal tunnel syndrome, birding compulsive
disorder? Why does the psychiatrist burst out crying when a sandhill
crane flies by? Why does the poet crawl into a sand dune to find a
snowy owl? The shrink is tired of fixing others, of misdiagnosing.
The poet is tired of being diagnosed and then misdiagnosed and then
diagnosed again. They know the most culpable are the normal ones
requiring normalcy from others.

Colibri

Wingspan of an owl.
Your heartbeat is the sky.
You hover over parliaments.
Then hurtle toward a new paradigm.
Ten primary wings, humming down the air.
Pollinator of the ineffable.
Consonants vowel away
into invisibles.
When Aztec warriors die in a battle,
they return to this earth as hummingbirds.
The abduction is an ancient wedding ritual.
And you courted the Invisible.

Notes from the Mental Aviary - X

Foucault offers a list of entries from various confinement registers:

- "of unsound mind"
- "obstinate plaintiff"
- "wicked cheat"
- "man who spends days and nights deafening others with his songs and shocking their ears with horrible blasphemy"
- "gruff, sad, unquiet spirit"
- "18th-century priest who practiced usury"

Thomas Szasz says we manufactured madness. What if it is both/and? Although the 20th century has been deemed "a psychiatric century," madness remains an inscrutable mystery, possibly divine.

A group of owls, herons, and hoopoes stormed through my window. They want to found a literary group. I will need to rent an amphitheatre.

I explain to them that in order to get funding they will need an eco name. They should write to Gary Snyder and ask him to pee on their banner in the moonlight. The Sierra Club might fund them. How about a parade topped by foghorns? Some of them are leaving for warmer countries. We added an attendance policy. The absent ones claimed they were getting sloppy drunk with Wisława Szymborska in Kraków.

A few days later, the cranes showed up. There were other birds called couplets that swung their pollinating eggs. A bird called "consonant" swarmed in, pouting, judgmental. He lifted himself in the air and swallowed the aphids. Then yellow phonemes (similar to warblers) rose slowly as in a balloon, and – the further they went – envisioned themselves as necessary.

There were gold-winged hyperboles thrusting around. Synecdoche stole cotton candy from a church bazaar and smoke came out of its belly, wafting like incense. Ellipses, outraged, isolated on trees, on strike. Coughing Chernobyl, displaying stigmas.

Herzog is coming next week to do a documentary. I consulted with the Chancellor of American Poets and a chief of the National Audubon Society to discuss this phenomenon. I am receiving funds.

Notes from the Mental Aviary - XI

Birds are daimons, *duende*, spiritual forces. They pollinate the boundary between the angelic and the demonic. The swan that rapes Leda is demonic. The sea-hawk that seizes Ahab's hat is savage.

In countless myths, the universe is hatched from an egg. In Ojibwa legends, it is a Loon who made the world. Ancient authors believed birds migrated to the Moon in winter. Storks bring babies; owls – death.

We have always imagined the dead as birds taking off, flying to heavens. In Gilgamesh, Enkidu dreams of the dead wearing feathers.

The soul as a winged creature.

In Christian paintings, a bird flies out of the mouth of a dying saint.

Iroquois set a bird free when a chief died.

Tiny Throat Diagnoses

Spring comes to the Galápagos, and you – blue-footed booby –
shuffle your feet awkwardly to ask out a female. You flap and wiggle
even as she refuses you.
Rejected, now you are exiled from paradise. You point to the sky. You
do not attempt to reduce or rationalize suffering, like Job's friends.

I was advised to recommend celibacy, but after you landed in my
window – while I was reading *Animal Madness* – I crossed it out
and hid you in my closet. You sat so quietly, unabashed – so much
innocence.

Your blue feet court transcendence.

When I come out of *my* closet, I will flap my blue feet.

Notes from the Mental Aviary - XII

For madness Hildegard recommends a warm loaf of organic bread
with a cross carved on top. She recites:
May God, who deprived the devil of every precious stone
after he had broken his commandments,
drive out from you, X
all phantasms and all magic spells,
and may he release you from all the pain of this madness.

Then eat the bread, those who suffer!

It will heal you.

Water and salt and leaven: to enliven. Hence, the healing power of
Communion.

If, on the other hand,

Hildegard writes,

you are oppressed by melancholy,
put onyx into your mouth.

We rub ashes on our bodies,
wear garlands to drive demons away;
we confuse God with gurus in saffron robes.

In Egyptian burial, *ka*—a tiny angel
departs the body, and death arrives.

Specks may be written down.

Notes from the Mental Aviary - XIII

For irregular behavior you will be sent to a house of correction

Carrie Buck was declared feebleminded and promiscuous. She had been raped by a relative of her foster parents. When she became pregnant, they sent her to a colony... She was sterilized in The Virginia State Colony for Epileptics and Feeble Minded.

70,000 forced sterilizations... In states like North Carolina, they targeted disproportionately black and poor women. They said it was an "appendectomy," as they cauterized the path of eggs toward fertilization.

American eugenics movement informed the Immigration Act of 1924 that favored northern and western Europeans over those from southern and eastern Europe, as well as all Asians.

The Nazis gassed schizophrenics.

Fight flight freeze

American bittern,
play freeze tag with me
till the sun sets & and you merge
with the reeds again.

Elongate your neck, sway,
the slow motion strutting
of a baron on parade.

Puff out your neck
& inflate your food pipe.

Skulk, duck
and preen –
I am mesmerized,
I follow you into the temple
of cattails and bulrushes.

We walk together stealthily
and you point your beak
into the sky and start hiccupping.

I chant your book of hours
at dusk, psalms of camouflage

Till I get my citizenship.
The ceremony is over,
And you fly off to another case.
The droplets of anthem
shine on my beak.

Tiny Throat Diagnoses

A sparrow hears calls. Confabulations? Delusions of grandeur? I sit her on my lap and lull her, with the aid of lavender crumbs, into hypnosis. Her voice now different: higher pitched, more melodious, oneiric.

To be an African Chief or Leopardi's shepherd,
to commune with the moon and sing;
to be in the fields where a calf is born,
to be a beggar or a duffle coat,
a bohemian smoking,
a seamstress,
or the grand camel who only has sand

I tell her of Plato and how he considered madness a gift. He divided madness into four types: the prophet, the poet, the mystic, and the lover. She could use her madness for prophecy and channel the calls into one calling, just like Elijah. She is enraptured; she gets a poopy diaper.

She tells me it's not in the wind that the call transpires. Nor a sparrow's favorite tree, nor in the flies the sparrow caught. Not even in the earthquake. Nor the draughts that came later.

A poem is a snowy owl. A vesper of dunes, a mystic of plumage. Follow its curve. Not a liturgy; rather, an auspicious crochet. Polar opposites: whiter than snow, spangled and streaked with black hieroglyphs, as if wings in flight.

It is a sacrament of dunes. It is not through our will that we receive. We must unearth ourselves. From beyond the dunes, the grass, the grace comes. We are left with maps, divinations, unanswered prayers. The burning bush, the apparition, a giant in a solitary field. The path is often twisted; it moves through labyrinths of negatives, misleading tropes, metonymies.

A snowy owl resides in a slippage. Momentarily, it glows on the shore. It contorts, throws up a pellet.

The poem, still angular with the bones of experience.

Notes from the Mental Aviary - XIV

(In the Post-Cartesian world, delirium became a body disorder. It was not the soul or mind, but the body –somaticism – the nervous system. Later on, the psychophysiological approach pioneered by Florentine doctor, Vincenzo Chiarugi, bridged the gap between Cartesian dualism: Chiarugi proposed the moral treatment of insanity.

But it was in fact a medieval Benedictine nun, Hildegard, who practiced a biopsychosocial approach to treating mental illness. This attempt at synthesis was later dismissed by the highly compartmentalized field of psychiatry. A noble woman, Sigewiza, in the lordly estate of St. Maximin's Abbey, was said to be possessed by evil spirits, and brought to Hildegard's monastery. They ate, prayed, sang, cooked, gardened, and played games together. Sigewiza became part of the sisterhood; Hildegard conversed regularly with the woman's demons. Forty days later, the day before Easter, Sigewiza was healed, but Hildegard became ill for the next forty days and was attacked by evil spirits who threatened her with death...)

Tiny Throat Diagnoses

I called the cactus wren into my office, as I was receiving many letters of complaint.

Why would he sneak into the nests of chickadees, bluebirds, and red-winged blackbirds to prick their eggs? Is he a greedy landlord evicting the birds? Does he have a Napoleon complex?

I almost sent him to a reformatory and stamped "vandalism" on my diagnostic sheet, but instead, I called a priest for an exorcism. Once I was told the demon had left, I put him into a blue Victorian cage and gave it to my friend. If he thrashes, give him some gummies with CBD.

A Poet and a Shrink (II)

How does the psychiatrist meet the poet? It starts in the mailbox. The shrink receives a letter from Saint Francis to please stop diagnosing the birds. "Do not pathologize my little creatures," he writes. "Do not catch a joy as it flies. Why do you fix them with your formulating phrases?"

"Sing of your self-imposed exiles! Where are the seeds of yesteryears? Shed the layers of your garments. Once you peel off your superego, you will arrive at the naked in you, the wounded, the poet. Remember when you were little, you composed lines of awe; you collected epiphanies."

It was a blackbird who composed the opening of the Rondo in Beethoven's "Violin Concerto." Its song has no repetition… it alters and shifts…a door ajar for new variations. Now the pace quickens, the *rubato* enters, the next day the different tune with tenuto and semitone. Notice it is all a music…*and & and & and*

Head-feathers ruffled, neck out-stretched. A caressing touch to an octave.

Another blackbird has a preference for Bach. But it prolongs its trills – squeaky notes at the end – a postmodern touch. The palimpsest of chuckle notes. Like Becket's characters transcribed to music.

A blackbird I met in Poland (so called *kos*) paraphrased Aeschylus, overheard from Boris Johnson (blackbirds steal from people, never from other birds):

For the rest I stay silent; a great ox stands upon my tongue – yet the nest, could it but sing, might hum a plain tale: since, for my part, by my own choice I have tunes for those who know, and for those who do not know, I have lost my song.

Great blackbird stands upon my tongue… For the rest I stay silent and I stop the prescriptions.

Long-wattled Umbrellabird
(Cephalopterus Penduliger)

Your wattle darkened the room. How grand it was; you swung it and
I could not help falling for you. You had a John Travolta pompadour.
You were more than a bird; you were a Werther. Your wattle wattled
for the sake of wattling.

And not to spill a single grain

My mother welcomes me
with half-empty sugar packets
in her palms. She takes them
for dollars.
They perch like fledglings;
the puffs of white grace
awaiting their take off
"Can I hold them?" I ask
and she slowly deposits them
into my hands.
Each grain of sugar
carries a trajectory
of longing.
Like the centrifugal leaps
of my mother's neurons
make her grasp the *inscape*
of things.
One needs to be an oracle
to hear an oracle.

Tiny Throat Diagnoses

A sparrow tired of being a sparrow. The injustices mount: "Little brown jobs" – ubiquitous and invisible. Always the same seed. Humans don't even bother to use their binoculars…Would anyone even please be able to notice that there are: the Bachman's Sparrow, Grasshopper Sparrow, Sharp-tailed Sparrow, Seaside Sparrow, Lark Sparrow, Olive Sparrow, Sage Sparrow, Chipping Sparrow, Clay-colored Sparrow, Fox Sparrow, Savannah Sparrow, and Vesper Sparrow.

With such names the sparrow could be a prophet. Then to her the songship, the twirl, the covenants would belong. Venerable Bede, in his Ecclesiastical History of the English People, says the soul is a sparrow that passes through the hall of a king.

Or, she could be the queen of kinkiness, just like a saltmarsh sparrow; each of her eggs in a nest with different DNA. She could be a powerful aphrodisiac. Nymphomaniac witches disguise themselves as sparrows.

In the meantime, I am giving her a short test. I am sprinkling crumbs:

Do you swing on branches?

Do you feel…

    a. Little to no interest in flying

    b. Guilt

    c. Lack of preference for lard

    d. Aversion to singing

    e. Desire to fly into glass windows

Do you prefer being called:

    a slut (William Carlos Williams)

    a "sad" sparrow (cliché)

    a pet of courtesans (Greeks)

    an "amorous" sparrow (Elizabeth Bishop)

Let's look at what you eat: What feeders do you frequent? It's a sunflower oil deficiency. I prescribe turmeric, which helps with inflammation. I prescribe Wordsworth, who wrote: "Man's life is like a sparrow, mighty King!" But, sad sparrow, first read Catullus, in which a girl keeps you tenderly on her lap.

Notes from the Mental Aviary - XV

The Flemish town Geel had, and still has, a foster system of inviting mentally afflicted people to live with local residents, sometimes for the rest of their lives—instead of separating the so-called healthy from the so-called sick. The tradition stretches back to the 13th century, when people would come to Geel on a pilgrimage to offer their mental afflictions to Saint Dymphna, the patron of mental breakdowns.

Tiny Throat Diagnoses

Royal Tern,
Your copulatory behavior leaves me speechless. You extend your neck
and whirl around like a skirt, and she turns, too, in a trance, while
your orange beak dominates her, or ruptures her. And then, when she
pauses – having second thoughts – you mount her and stay forever.
For most other avians it is a matter of seconds – you stand on her
shoulders while looking onto the sea. Four minutes pass; then you
take her from behind and push your tail under hers. Lordy, lordy,
lordy. After the physical affair the symbolic starts: You bring your
lady a fish. You start again: neck extended, head high towering over
her and wings folded as if a minuet.

She starts whirling again. The whole thing culminates in the long and
plump fish. She won't take a small one.

They perch on electric wires. What larks! Leather, cocktails, chatter, screeches – courting and mating; flaps and frills. Radiant and wired. Socialites and tightrope walkers on massive pylons carrying Eversource's main 345-kilovolt transmission lines.

Subtle networks of cross-codes.

If you ask, "What the beak are you doing here?" the birds trill back, "That's how you meet your mate!" But with time the voltage gets to them. They have sweatier wings, then they start experiencing *déjà vu* – the same bar scene, the same song, the same birdwatchers down below. Groundhog Day.

Their dorsal ventricular ridge gets affected. They wobble slightly and get blurred vision.

It is hard for winged creatures to face limits. So they pluck their feathers and dissociate. Some stare past the horizon; some fall to their deaths...

Others turn to divinities: ancient birds, avian prophets. Their wings flutter more and tremble. Their sadness acquires a richness, as if escalated from this finite electrical line to a higher level.

Wired birds, your brains are built of small clumps – like clouds. No cortex. If the clumps are affected from slow radiation, you will rain the rays back on us.

Notes from the Mental Aviary - XVI

(Because natural dyes were costly, chemists looked for alternatives. That's how methylene blue was discovered; and the molecule "phenothiazine" was an inherent ingredient of this compound – and was used in antipsychotics and antidepressants. Lithium salts were tested first on guinea pigs. It was introduced as the first psychotropic in 1949, replacing amphetamines.

Valium was the most prescribed tranquilizer in the 1960's. Prozac was taken by 8 million people within five years. Slowly the divide between sane and insane became fuzzier… Some mental institutions closed and compulsory treatment was almost abolished.

Still, the pharmaceuticals are in our rivers, soil, and carcasses. Birds eat antidepressants.)

A Poem

Of Aunt Anielka
or rather a woman in a black scarf
who taught me how to kiss chicks
by passing my saliva
into their beaks.

Of Aunt Anielka
or rather a woman with mulberry and jasmine blossoms
who each night would sleep in her clothes
in case she'd have to flee
the Germans.

Of Aunt Anielka
or rather a woman who inscribed icons in me
until the swallows in willows wept
and my words clasped
luminous shells.

Notes from Mental Aviary - XVII

Plato compares a philosopher to a bird:

"The mind of the philosopher alone has wings… He is like a bird fluttering and looking upward and careless of the world below; and he is therefore thought to be mad."

Socrates calls the bird's wing: "the corporeal element most akin to the divine."

Birds point to transcendence, divinity.

Coleridge likens imagination to the flight of starlings. Birds are clouds of winged songs (W.S. Merwin). For Wallace Stevens *The wild warblers* […] are *the lustrous inundations.*
Coleridge envisions a white albatross as an archangel: *Methought I peeped to secrets which took hold of God.*

The Holy Spirit is portrayed as a bird. It descends as a dove and impregnates the Virgin Mary through her ear. St Teresa of Avila saw the vision of a dove whose wings were made of tiny luminous shells.

If the Holy Spirit is God, could God be a bird? In Judaism, Yahweh is an eagle, protecting Jacob. In Christianity, eagles and phoenixes symbolize Christ. Pelicans are a symbol of Christ. European goldfinches appear on countless paintings of the Madonna with Child.

Tiny Throat Diagnoses

He flew into my office, meowing. To identify with his enemy?
Stockholm syndrome?

No, it's Thomas Jefferson's favorite: the mockingbird. "Four Hundred
Tongues"... Hopi Indians fed a mockingbird tongue to their children
to facilitate the learning of traditional tribal songs.

Is he full of dybbuks?

Why not just say he's a polyglot? Or maybe the Holy Spirit descended
with the gift of tongues?

He creates pastiches, mistranslations. He mimics.

When does mimicry become interpretation? A translator is a mis-
translator. A fraud? Sound burglar? Twenty robberies per minute!

In the Middle Ages, "translatio" meant the theft or removal of holy
relics from one monastery to another. 14th-century Kabbalists called
translation "ha'atagah," which also meant transmigration. So the
mockingbird might have been a cat in his previous life or a shrink.

Can one convey an organ tune on a trombone?

Goethe says only a poet can be a good translator of poetry. Only a
musical bird can translate other birds.

A Poet and a Shrink (III)

This is how formal intent dissolves and voices conflate. They meet
and swap names. They swap titles and credentials. They swap
prescriptions. One pill for grammar, two pills for Pulitzer. They flush
the pills down the toilet. They appeal the bill. They come out of their
closets flapping their feet. This is how formal intent peels away.
They swap their patients. English is now the patient; it suffers from
imbalance. How do you do... what? The guinea pig is not from
New Guinea and is not a pig. Quicksand is not quick. Let's stamp:
"delusional."

Difference Between Snuggling and Cuddling

"Cuddle" is an ancient word. The Mesopotamians used to cuddle their cows. In Middle English, it was more like *couth*. In Old Dutch it was *kudden* – to flock together.
Today, you can buy a cuddle.
(https://snugglebuddies.com/pricing)

"Snuggling," on the other hand, comes from a tiny creature called a *snug* and should not be confused with *smuggling*, which comes from another creature called a *smug*.
You could, however, *smuggle a snuggle*.

Snuggle has an older sister, "nestle." Old English *nestlian*: to "build a nest." The alternative of snuggling is to drink *Nestle*. In that way, you build a tiny nest inside your body that might accrue to the size of a mogul. This condition will turn you into a ptarmigan: a permanent snuggle.

Soul in Egyptian hieroglyphs
is a long-legged stone
plover that cries
at night to sanctify
each pebble.

Hibou Blanc Speaks

I curl my feathers, as if bowing before divinities. They congregate
with masks and big, pointed pistols, and they *click click click*. Is this
Armageddon? I greet them like an archangel before virgins...

I announce a truce. Three hours pass; eternity – for me. We partake in
a one-sided ritual; I am bored. Up to my eyeballs. Whatever a retina
receives must be twice as bright for me. My eardrums, bombarded
by the clicking, become delirious grasshoppers. Oy. Whoosh. I clack,
they click.

Some of them fall on their knees. They leave stretchmarks on my soul.
They are smoke in my nostrils.

There is a short woman crawling toward me. I am a white cloud. She
is Baba Yaga. Is she giving me an Eskimo hug? Is that a mouse in
her pocket or a kitten? Perhaps, she just looks for mist to disperse
my secrets. She whispers with uncanny accents...*sówko, sóweczko,
mamko*. I yawn. Why can't she just love her jays and chickadees? She
looks fixated, obsessed, mad.

They confuse me with the Holy Grail. They want me to save them
from oblivion. I am just a refugee in the dunes, a facsimile of the
tundra. I, too, pine for the original, a primal. I want to make traces in
the sand, not be a trophy bird. Or a prop of a bird, a plush sweet toy
with fluffy slippers on. I hunt, eat, rest, excrete, and vomit pellets. Yet
they want me to be the answer for their infinite thirst.

Will they not let me go until I bless them? A voice of one crying out.
Meanwhile, they stalk. Leaving pellets is not safe.

I will not deliver you from nothingness. When you quiet all the
turmoil, look for a bird with a freshly plucked olive branch.

Notes from the Mental Aviary - XVIII

(Humans are both angelic and demonic. A virgin and a monster. We
rescue birds and we make them extinct. We admire and enslave them.
Out of love, we possess them. For the sake of taxonomy, Audubon
shot bird species, including countless Carolina parakeets. Thoreau
admitted to eating red-headed woodpeckers. He described broiling
a passenger pigeon. We are egg collectors, plumage hunters. We
stalk beauty, we wound it. A bird is booty, it helps us affirm our tax
deductible duties.)

Tiny Throat Diagnoses

Western Bowerbird, you came in your pickup to show me your bower.
When I left for the restroom, you scoured for shells.

You were trying to please your partner. Hence, your open-floor plan
style, using tchotchkes: human nails, bits of string, marbles, dung,
shells, bottle caps, and a Barbie doll.

A female struts around your house, while you pick up shiny objects,
waving them before her, fanning your crest. To no avail. You remain a
bachelor in nuptial plumage. Then, you rearrange the ornaments for
the next female and position yourself beside them (so-called forced
perspective).

Bowerbird, you subvert your own needs to please picky partners. You
feather around, making sacrifices to flatter their needs. We need to
get you back on an even keel. No more decorations to impress your
friends. Donate these to charity.

I put some on my Christmas tree.

The Anglo-Saxon bird can sell any of its chicks under the age of one.
The remaining chicks are allowed to drink beer with their meals. If
a headache occurs, they peck holes in their own heads to release evil
spirits.

Every Thursday, it disguises itself as a medieval minstrel to spy on
the Vikings. Its song is one or two syllables; it has to preserve energy
to hide from humans. Humans eat only twice a day and sell their
children under seven.

The Anglo-Saxon bird fantasizes of feasting on humans, sucking out
their eyes and skulls. He has no video games. He sings riddles instead.
Sonorous songs, that's how the birds bond.

The Anglo-Saxon bird tells riddles to humans to delay being eaten.
Today, they have grilled a hedgehog and a cat instead. Their crops are
never enough. Magic spells and chants don't help.

His turn might be tomorrow, so he asks:

I fold my head and I lift up my legs. I am a transparent ball. A
perching vitamin. What am I?

When is a wolf an herb?

They Are Always Running Afoul of the Rules

To wit:

Aggression, theft, abandonment of parents, pecking and scratching the tourists, plucking the eyes from baby seals, attacking whales. Herring gulls, kelp gulls, gulls of the sea – were made for play and infamy. They stamp their feet to imitate rainfall and trick earthworms to come up, just for fun. They stand on the road and drop oysters so the cars can crack them.

The ocean is their promise. They dwell in waves. The ocean pulsates with sea cucumbers, anemones, the moody pools of diatoms, sponges and isopods. Curious weeds, pelagic beards and the stories of tides and sea potatoes. The Kingfisher seeks the silence of the ocean. Life accrues and so do mangroves, periwinkles and limpets. All is fluid; grace and grief – sea lettuce, eelgrass, kelp, driftwood and shells, and a grain of sand, with a liquid shield around it. Marsh grasses absorb the gulls' sins.

On the other hand, naked fat bodies – munching on fish and chips. So the gulls swoop down to shear off pieces of flesh. They are hooligans. More misunderstood than Frost's "The Road Not Taken."

Our hands hold little boats of protein, tiny metonymies of ocean. Hence, their settling for less: a piece of sandwich or an ear. The reawakened desire, unfulfilled, turns to violence. They love clashing with humanity. And they do us service! Beauty has teeth and terrifies.

Elegy for Stolen Poppies

He pinched the poppies from a war memorial and will make a nest.
The poppies are red; they envelop the pigeon – they hypnotize.

The poppy pigeon pays the tribute of tributes.

His grandfather, Cher Ami, was a carrier pigeon who flew through
gunfire, with a bullet in its chest, blinded in one eye, missing a leg –
to deliver a message that saved the lives of 194 soldiers.

Transcending trauma and grief, veiled in red and oneiric, he will
bring forth his offspring in a nest of poppies.
The *paparazzi* are already there. Soon he is on Le Monde and BBC
One.

His children will want to be grateful. Their droppings will be precious
fertilizers. In pigeon vocabulary, both poopies and poppies are sacred.

In Flanders' fields the poppies blow

I follow the shoal of silver pigeons. They look like magnetized
minnows in the sky. My grandmother gave me a poppy when I cried.
I would suck on it and go to sleep. A pre-war pacifier in Poland.

Can you navigate a place you have never visited?

Whisper through an eggshell
ka, a tiny winged spirit, in Egyptian burial,
will whisper back
I will meet you when the morning
meets the meadow.

Notes from the Mental Aviary - XIX

"The stork in the heaven knoweth her appointed times" – Jeremiah.

Migrating cranes mark winter and they tell farmers when to plough again (Hesiod, *Works and Days*). "Contemplate" derives from *templum*, an Etruscan custom of observing the flight of birds to look for one's destiny.

In Ancient Greece and Rome, "auspices" – Latin *avis* (birds) + *spicere* (look at) – was a science. "Augury" meant looking at the entrails of birds. In Ancient Rome, a College of Augurs was instituted; affairs of state were for the birds. Hence, the term *aves admittant* – "the birds allow it." After all, it was the geese of Juno's temple that saved Rome… And it was quails that saved the Israelites in the desert.

Today in New England, we examine the thickness of a goose's feathers to predict the coming winter.

The hummingbird is a loner with a tendency to overthink.
Biologically speaking, it has the largest brain per body size. The
largest heart, too. And a third eyelid! It reads a lot. But it uses
its tongue, micro pumps, to scoop up the lines and to underline
important passages.

Hummingbirds prefer poetry for its power of ellipsis. Poetry does
not describe; it reenacts. They are like the French Symbolists; they
do not like Mary Oliver; they need poetry inscrutable to the masses.
They like hermetic texts. They get so excited about deciphering lines
of poetry, they have to munch all the time, mostly sucking on sugar.
That's why their wings flap 50 times per second; they have to manage
intensity. It is like having fifty epiphanies per second. In fact, over-
epiphanized, they suffer from chronic fatigue; that's when they fly
inside our houses and freeze. That's how we know they overdosed on
grace and God.

Notes from the Mental Aviary – XX

DSM:

1952, 128 pages, 106 diagnoses

2000, 943 pages (diagnoses including mathematics disorder and caffeine addiction)

2013, 265 diagnoses

Some of the new labels:

- "cannabis withdrawal"

- "internet gaming disorder"

- "premenstrual dysphoric disorder"

- "hoarding disorder"

- "restless leg syndrome."

Psychiatry is a mockingbird; it has four hundred tongues.
The pathologizing tunes proliferate.

Cosmetic psychopharmacology has emerged: we take medications to become "better than well."

Some Consider Intellectualization a Form of Dissociation

The Dodo is disillusioned with nature; nature is fallen. He reads Schopenhauer and contemplates sin. He is working a thesis about extinction. He's agonizing over it. He is smart, not ludicrous. Not a quirk of nature. But he has no kids and, like Diogenes, spends his days in a dry tub (asterisk: a bird bath without water). Typically, after having a breakfast of seeds, bulbs, roots and crabs, he disagrees with Aristotle that only man is a *zoon mimeticon*. What about his relatives: carrier pigeons, flying amidst bombs to deliver messages, or symbolizing peace? What about his brother crows, holding a funeral on the highway for dead colleagues? He doesn't enumerate all the examples; they are countless.

He is, however, more friendly to Spinoza's *conatus*, striving to survive.

The Dodo's ghost editorial:

I can't fly but I do not lack the art of recollection. My great-great grandparents told me how, 500,000 years ago, they flew with the other dodos under the marigold moon. Full of grace, they were still small and agile. But Mother Nature made us fat – we grew double chins, then love handles, then flightless, clumsy, and ludicrous bodies. Nature betrayed us. No kids. That's how we turned to philosophy. Disappointed by humans, we started to pray to the Dodo God. And when we resurrect, we will be slim and full of flight. There will be a marigold moon again, and offspring. I am an epigone, but I am not intellectualizing. Or, if I am dissociated, it is due to all the preconceptions you have made about me. What dodos!

A poem is hiding in the bark of a tree. Sometimes it falls out and suffers a concussion.

A poem is a bird's glow. Nanometers, not enough to know.

A poem is a chick with ultraviolet light around its beak so we know where to place worms.

A poem is an owl with fluorescent wings. Imagine how their new lines glow.

A poem is a dove with a freshly plucked olive branch, to take us home. We need to search for it with blacklight. Its wings glow raspberry pink or blue and lavender. Together our gazes glow.

Oh owl, oh burning bush, drop a message on our parchment of birches!

Notes from the Mental Aviary - XXI

(In myths and folklore, changing into birds is a sudden halting of—or veto to—the chain of unbearable events.

Alcyon, in Ovid's *Metamorphoses*—upon seeing the drowned body of her shipwrecked husband, turns into a kingfisher "and thrusts her growing beak between his lips."

In *The Street of Crocodiles* by Bruno Schulz, a father who is a breeder and collector of exotic birds slowly turns into one. His eyes mist over, his arms waving as wings; his lips emit a bird's call.

Julian Barnes, in *Flaubert's Parrot*, mentions the true story of a man who taught his pet bird to pronounce the name of his diseased beloved. Upon the parrot's death, the man believed himself to be a parrot, and even escaped from an asylum to perch on a tree before being recaptured.

In William Wharton's *Birdy*, a teenage boy hopes to develop muscles that will enable him to fly. Birdy enjoys a dream life as a bird, but when it is disrupted, he winds up in mental hospitals.

Birds are the mad earth's missionaries.)

Delusions of Reference

Dear Ewa Chrusciel,

The council of birds has met to discuss your identity. We have read
your musings. We have conducted interviews. We have perched
on your family tree. We found out that you are related to us. After
further research, we are convinced you belong to a species of wading
birds, the rail family, the larger family of Gruiform, "crane-like." We
sent our representative to Poland who discovered that your last name,
Chrusciel, signifies us: the family of gallinule. Just to let you know,
the members of your species have purple-blue plumage that shines
green and turquoise in good lighting. Adults have a blue shield on
their forehead, which extends to a red and yellow bill. Your brownish
colors are due to the fact that your family got derailed and displaced
during the second war of birds. You ended up in the wrong climate
and a heavy diet of cabbage, pierogi, potatoes, and cheese-cake
has caused your anthropomorphization. With a good diet, flying
and singing lessons, and some avian unconditional love (we are
polygamous), you will be able to ascend to the ranks of a rail. Our
avian physician will propose adding a combination of two pigments:
melanins and *lipochromes* to your entrails. For now, we recommend
wading and diving for food. In the end, you will be our ambassador,
since you have no chance to survive in the wild.
FYI, your extended family is comprised of 14 species of large cranes,
145 species of smaller crakes and rails, as well as other varieties of
birds: limpkins and trumpeters. Furthermore, kagu and sunbittern
are your exotic relatives. Your most remote ancestor is a great
Diatryma of Eocene days, a primitive crane. *Noblesse Oblige.*

In a nutshell: You are cured! Eat some bread and do some belly
dancing. Follow the curve of a dove; the twig in its beak has a
message, from your true family.
Don't let the screen door hit you on the way out.
Yours,
Purple Gallinule

Tiny Throat Revelations

Growing up in Poland, I was taught to stigmatize mental illness. I internalized Wisława Szymborska's poem "Advertisement," where a psychiatric pill speaks like the devil and entices a human to sell her soul to pharmaceuticals.

When I moved to the United States, I began to understand how crucial psychiatric medications can be in saving people's lives. Yet even here, mental illness is often stigmatized through hyper-classification. T.S. Eliot expresses this in "Love Song of Alfred J Prufrock" by the image of eyes which pigeonhole a human being until it is pinned and wriggling on the wall like a captured butterfly.

Here in these poems, my psychiatrist undergoes a series of conversions as she realizes that the point is not to classify thoughtlessly, but to "make music instead," to dwell in astonishment. As the eponymous protagonist of Fyodor Dostoevsky's novel, *The Idiot*, proclaims: "I believe the world will be saved by beauty."

Here, birds evade the anthropomorphization of psychiatrists – and of poets – when psychiatrist and poet become one. Thus, the anthropomorphization goes in reverse, and the human being becomes "other," more avian. Like Noah's dove, it proclaims a new covenant, with a twig in its beak and a message: "We are all mad; some more than others, but no one is spared the affliction. And the madder we are, the more sacred."

May we each find the way to strive for humor, beauty, humanity, and most of all balance in loving and embracing the world.

CODA

Bird Symposium

Location: Metropolitan Pavilion NY, NY (125 West 18th street)

Instructions:
Cereal boxes to be hung in the auditorium, so the birds can roost.
Seeds to be stashed in the chairs where birds are free to peck.
Caterpillars, worms, and feathers spread liberally for nibbling and
play.

Human participants allowed to attend, after being screened for slings,
arrows, and cats.

Keynote speaker: Raven Edgar Corvus Corax

Title: The Effect of Electromagnetic Fields on Birds' Fertility.
6 AM EST, Main Auditorium

Aesthetic Panel:
Birds of Paradise, Hyacinth Macaw, Quetzal, Red Crested Turaco,
Golden Pheasant, Bower
Topics:
- Flying buttresses in the evolution of sparrow colonization
- Crenellation design for birds and humans
- Pigeon-spike placement: a bird's eye view
- The most spectacular skyscrapers to visit on migration
- Nest architecture
- Best male skirts and feather dyes

History and anthropology seminar
Title: How Many Roasted Sparrows Have You Eaten?

Synopsis:
Mao Zedong named sparrows in the Four Pests Campaign. Posters
of bright-eyed children and dead sparrows. Sparrows poisoned, their
eggs crushed. Genocide. Then the locusts showed up. By 1960 all the
crops were destroyed. 30 million dead humans.

Literature Panel:
NOTE: Due to reduced funds for literature, we have only one speaker:
the nightingale. The next planned speaker, the phoenix, is waiting in the
wings.

Title: The Nightingale in "Ode to a Nightingale"

Open beak reading:
2 AM EST

Sample improvisation: Lark and lyrebird

The spring came
to mean everything and nothing,
despite the forsythia

Linden linden linden
Larch trees weep
Ginkgoes speak in yellow

Oaks grieve
over their clichés
Where, the seeds of yesteryear?
Where is the cat?

The sap leaks into
spells, frail & solitary
in underground rivers.

Sing of your exiles
in olive trees

Willow, sing of Desdemona
Willow trees, willows
are damned literary

Drumming Circle:
Flickers, Hummingbirds, and the Cockatoo with a Mohawk

SEED-TIME BREAK

3 AM panel – Survival Working Group: (Bubo Virginianus,
Cooper's Hawk, and others from the family Accipitridae TBA)
Topic: How to reduce detection by minimizing shadows

Trauma Working Group Panel: Daily 1-2 AM EST
Eligible birds include:
- Birds that were/are stoned
- Birds who were fed vegan caterpillars and worms
- Birds who nested in plastic bags hanging in trees
- Birds who nested in bras hanging on ski lifts
- Birds who chewed through electric wires
- Birds who flew into glass windows
- Birds that tried to eat seeds tossed on anti-pigeon spikes
- Birds who got stuck in ventilating systems
- Birds who got stuck in tar
- Birds who choked on fertilizers
  Eligibility applications available in Main Auditorium

Linguistic Panel:
*Qur'ān: "And Solomon was David's heir. And he said, O mankind! Lo!
we have been taught the language of the birds (ullimnā manṭiq aṭ-ṭayr)
and have been given abundance of all things" (27:16).*

I
Workshop: **Kookaburra (moderator),** Lyrebird, Mockingbird,
Parrots, Starlings.
Time and Place: TBA
Title: How to mimic a chainsaw, car alarm, and flushing toilet
Fee: A pound of hemp seeds or two pounds of lard

II
Title: Bilingualism in birds: A comparative approach to birdsong and
language development
Speaker: Goldfinch

III
Title: Boycott Manifesto

- Instead of killing two birds with one stone, we propose to feed them a scone.
- The bird in the hand is worth two in the bush? No! All birds in the bushes!
- Cut your hand if it tempts you to hold a bird in hand
- Do not catch a bird as it flies…
- A vile nonsense to consider birds as penises. Abolish!

Wellness group
Topics:
- Narcolepsy in Birds
- Monogamy vs. polygamy – pros and cons

LARD BREAK

Clairvoyant Group
Keynote speaker: Elaenia, a visionary

Synopsis:
I saw pigeons impaled on anti-nesting spikes
I saw anarchist Cockatoos throwing off anti-nesting spikes
I saw homeless people lying on anti-homeless spikes

I was a master, an engineer of spikes
laughing silently, or loudly, with other engineers
and for their feathers and furs, we cast a lot

None of it lasted
But the anarchy of white feathers
like a Dominican monk praying
like dervishes dancing
uprooting and rooting in the clouds
swaddling us in spikes

CATERPILLAR BREAK

98

Germophobe Working Group
(Registration closed)
Generosity Working Group

- Rules and tips for avian adoption
- Issues Forum: *Can humans be adopted?*

Environmental Working Group
Topics:
- How to survive winter: landfills of Morocco
  - o   Facilitator: a stork
- How to bring down planes
  - o   Trainer: a starling
- Cleaning beaches of human food waste
  - o   Field Demonstration: a gull

Divination Group (Canadian Geese)

If you see pine siskins giggling in the sky
Your next life will be chaotic
yet exuberant
Your days whimsically veering
hither and thither

Final Gala Ventriloquist Improvisation -- Curl-Crested Manucode

Speaking in the stomach begins...
A throat and a relic invoke a chorus
the memory of what hovers
under overcast skies. Feathery chandeliers,
baby throats sing softer, mere puffs of feather.

Each bird to its own craft. Snowies fast forty days to decipher the
grasses in dunes. Woodpeckers are the typewriter type: tapping their
obsessions meticulously. They end up with stigmata in their skull.
We need to shed
layer
after
layer

to peel back the "midrash."

They will meet us when then morning meets
        the meadow.
                      Emerald doves
                        will sing of
Trobrianders.

                       their throat tips ink-stained.

Reception to follow.
Swedish style buffet with a belly dancer.

Beaknotes:

A baby titmouse
is a tribute to Len Howard who dedicated her life to observing birds as individuals, especially titmice. The poem was inspired by her memoir: Birds as Individuals.
It is, in a sense, a persona poem, attempting to inhabit Howard' voice.

I write of Aunt Anielka
A loose adaptation of my poem written originally in Polish and translated into English by Karen Kovacik.

Swallows
Bob Dylan, "Subterranean Homesick Blues."

In myths and folklore
Ted Hughes "Skylark."

Bibliography

Glover, Morrill Allen. *Birds and Their Attributes*. NY, NY: Dover Publication; 1962.
Schulz, Bruno. *The Street of Crocodiles and Other Stories*. NY, NY; Penguin Books, 2008.
Lutwack, Leonard. *Birds in Literature,* Gainesville, Florida: University Press of Florida, 1994.
Ackerman, Jennifer. *The Genius of Birds*. Penguin Press, NY; 2016.
Burton, Robert. *Bird Behavior*. Alfred A Knopf, 1985.
Couzens, Dominic. *Extreme Birds*. Firefly Books, 2011.
Diagnostic and Statistical Manual of Mental Disorders. Fifth Edition. DSM- 5 American Psychiatric Association. 2018.
Foucault, Michel. *Madness and Civilization: A History of Insanity in the Age of Reason*. Vintage, 1988.
Phillips, Suzanne M; Boivin, Monique D. *Philosophy, Psychiatry & Psychology* : PPP; Baltimore Vol. 14, Iss. 4, (Dec 2007): 359-368,381-382. MEDIEVAL HOLISM: Hildegard of Bingen on Mental Disorder.
Hildegard of Bingen. *Selected Writings: Hildegard of Bingen*. London, England; Penguin Books, 2001.

Hildegard of Bingen. *Holistic healing,* trans. M. Pawlick, and P. Madigan, ed. M. Palmquist, and J. Kulas. Collegeville, MN: The Liturgical Press, 1994.

Berger, M. *On Natural Philosophy and Medicine: Selections from Causae et curae.* Cambridge: D. S. Brewer, 1999.

Roy, Porter. *Madness; A Brief History.* NY, NY; Oxford UP, 2002.

Feathery Thanks

Grateful acknowledgment is made to the following journals and anthologies for inviting the following poems from the book to perch on their pages:

Tipi di Ensemble (Anthology of Ensemble Press)
ALONE TOGETHER: Love, Grief, and Comfort During the Time of COVID-19 (ebook anthology)
Big Other
Spoon River Review
Washington Square Review
Solstice
Adirondack Review

I am grateful for Omnidawn Press whose editors, Rusty Morrison and Ken Keegan, continue to weave nests for my verses.

Particular thanks to my husband, Eric DeLuca, whose editorial and creative prowess never ceases to astound me.

Equal gratitude to Craig Greenman, a writer and philosopher, whose editing skills are brilliant.

I also want to thank my fellow-poets from two poetry groups:
Anny Jones, George Chase, Nancy Stewart, Ivy T. Schweitzer, Lisa Furmanski, Jeff Friedman. Without their inspirations, suggestions, and edits these poems would hardly ever truly hatch and fledge.

I am also grateful to Sally Asher, my friend and neighbor who would pop in to my house during the pandemic and help me with the editing process.

Thanks to Doug McDonald, my neighbor in Wilmot, NH, who built bluebird boxes in our garden.

Thanks to bluebirds who chose our garden for their nesting dreams. Thanks to hummingbirds visiting in the summer. To goldfinches, to wrens, juncos, barred owls, nuthatches, chickadees, downy woodpeckers keeping me company all Fall and winter while the book was being written. Thanks to snowy owl spending winter on Plum Island in MA for announcing necessary visions.

photo: Curtis White

Ewa Chrusciel's previous books in English are *Of Annunciations* (Omnidawn 2017), *Contraband of Hoopoe* (Omnidawn 2014), *Strata* (Emergency Press 2009, reprinted by Omnidawn in 2018). Her book *Contraband of Hoopoe* was translated into Italian by Anna Aresi and came out in Italy with Edizioni Ensemble in May 2019. Chrusciel also published three books in Polish: *Furkot* (2001), *Sopiłki* (2009), and *Tobołek* (2016). Her poems appeared in numerous journals and anthologies in USA, Italy, and Poland. She also translated into Polish: *White Fang* by Jack London, *The Shadow Line* by Joseph Conrad, and *More Stories from My Father's Court* by Isaac Bashevis Singer, as well as the book of selected poems by Jorie Graham, and selected poems of Kazim Ali, Lyn Hejinian, Cole Swensen and other American poets into Polish. She is an Associate Professor of Humanities at Colby-Sawyer College.

Yours, Purple Gallinude
I. ... Chiracal

Cover art by NanceSepe

Cover & pages: Avenir
Interior, perpetua: Adobe Minion Pro & Myriad Pro

Interior design by Ken Keegan

Printed in the United States
by Bookit International, Dulles, Virginia
On Sea Charlifter B19 Antique 360 rpi
Acid Free Archival Quality, Recycled Paper

Publication of this book was made possible in part by gifts from
Katherine & John Gravendyk in honor of Hillary Gravendyk,
Francesca Bell, Mary MacKey, and The New Place Fund.

Omnidawn Publishing
Oakland, California
Staff and Volunteers, Spring 2022

Rusty Morrison & Ken Keegan, senior editors & co-publishers
Laura Joakimson, production editor and poetry & fiction editor
Rob Hendricks, editor for Omniverse, poetry & fiction, &
post-pub marketing
Sharon Zetter, poetry editor & book designer
Jeff Kingman, copy editor
Liza Flum, poetry editor
Anthony Cody, poetry editor
Jason Bayani, poetry editor
Gail Aronson, fiction editor
Jennifer Metsker, marketing assistant
Jordyn MacKenzie, marketing assistant
Sophia Carr, marketing assistant

Yours, Purple Gallinule
Ewa Chrusciel

Cover art by Nancy Sepe

Cover typeface: Avenir
Interior typefaces: Adobe Minion Pro & Myriad Pro

Interior design by Ken Keegan

Printed in the United States
by Books International, Dulles, Virginia
On 55# Glatfelter B19 Antique 360 ppi
Acid Free Archival Quality Recycled Paper

Publication of this book was made possible in part by gifts from
Katherine & John Gravendyk in honor of Hillary Gravendyk,
Francesca Bell, Mary Mackey, and The New Place Fund

Omnidawn Publishing
Oakland, California
Staff and Volunteers, Spring 2022

Rusty Morrison & Ken Keegan, senior editors & co-publishers
Laura Joakimson, production editor and poetry & fiction editor
Rob Hendricks, editor for Omniverse, poetry & fiction, &
post-pub marketing,
Sharon Zetter, poetry editor & book designer
Jeff Kingman, copy editor
Liza Flum, poetry editor
Anthony Cody, poetry editor
Jason Bayani, poetry editor
Gail Aronson, fiction editor
Jennifer Metsker, marketing assistant
Jordyn MacKenzie, marketing assistant
Sophia Carr, marketing assistant